RED EYE

1973   **2013**   **Test Centre**

Iain Sinclair   RED EYE

Better even than red which, at moments, can be too manic.
Douglas Oliver, *The Harmless Building*

The moonsaw's come, the rainy night is milk, red eyes sea.
Jack Kerouac, *Visions of Cody*

Clay-songs of meat science, out from London,
for Michael McClure and Stan Brakhage

CORONAL WINDOW BREATHING

sun detached
by will of virus, by window

blind limps, faint knocking

cat's spasm pukes an orange stream
on to the porch (segmented rubber)

screened noises unpick my spine
penpoint moves by slow impulse

clay of my hands runs white
water reunites with water

mistakes in the text inviolate

▪

along one contour
a rose of light is suggested
radiant & kinetic

the other has been occulted
fear

is behind the expression
of approval

length of thigh / is wonder

▪

SOUR MILK EYE

saucer left by cat
two nights on the tiles

SPIRALS, CUTS, & RAISES
fur of acrid
but domestic POISON

THE BABY HAS CHEWED OFF
CHARLIE CHAPLIN'S FOOT, BUT THIS
IS NOT DISTRESSING, AND CONTAINS
NO HINT OF CARDBOARD GANGRENE

searching always for the phyletic,
the underlay of old behaviours

SHE BUILDS FROM US: our
house, & grid of routines, so
strange, now, to look upon

Light stopped down; no movement.
A grey membrane envelope.
In this set
small pains are the only register of colour.
The vein-blue of our daughter's eyelid rim
matching Anna's own.
The reddish patches inside her elbows.
She has inherited through us
her visceral palette. Bears gum
in snarl of first noises.
Without light, no other energy manifest.

'Light / is what your life is'

Post-coital rushes, plasmic spasms
in drift: a different quality, unlocked.

Fish shadows, shreddings.

STAR SHIRT: a cloud of intelligences
causing lockjaw, mind's sorry
rumour. And searched out coeval runes
that made themselves known.
If that would not crack the case
release the crabs from Victoria Station
into attendant one-night hotels.

A city disease.
Cloud torpedoes drop, shift,
curtain the skyshaft
with longwave colour variables, constant
lightleak: so
that true darkness (blackfield) seeps through
between tower blocks & mustard houses.

Such is their sensitivity
(his, worked for / hers, birthskin)
that the whole night dome is a map
& registers every affliction
in scale, low as it is.
The body dance interprets
space weathering
as varieties of asthma, dermotic imperfections,
uneven brain flux, and egg allergy
might be the medium of transmission.

And, again, she turns her head, astonished
he brushes fire flies out of his hair
disturbing the morning dimness.

Sleep is a slow skewer, driving in.
For him, work promises.

Bees of anger burn against her cheek.

'& dying is still... the "reason" why he does it'

      slate melt, the sky.
close close, this untropic thunder.
anchored in sweat to a northern rib,
the house groans, close close
to self-greasing. baby grows a splint
in this same thick vein of time.
          a rock-split, close to lightning.
          plates oiled, the charge
          bolts into earth.

      grey shield, no comfort.
pink sacks of horse manure
have not yet been banked
heated to straw for mushrooms.
          Oat-grey, not liquid.

      & bends away to
my notation of these details:
                      weather.

      rain ceremony
      responded to, not enforced.

THE ROOM

INCENSE OF DYING FLIES, SECRETIONS.
BLACK'D GLASS PLATES. AS IT WERE
STICKY TOBACCO SMOKE. THE DEATH OF ALL THINGS
BUILDS UP A GRID OF ODOURS
INTO WHICH WE WALK, WALLS RINGING,
HUNG WITH INFINITE REGRESSIVE BELLS.

SUNLIGHT: REACHES FOR CAMERA AGAINST
THE FORCING OF THIS FIRST SONG
THE BABY MAKES OUT OF CONFLICT & RESPONSE,
SOFTENING ROAR, ORCHESTRATED
WITH GESTURES OF ARM & HAND: CRAWL OUT
AWAY FROM CRADLE TOWARDS
AFTERNOON GRASS. NO ABSOLUTES OF HEAT.

UP TO A POINT, NO FURTHER.
CERTAIN INSISTENCES AGAINST SLEEP
THAT SEA WHICH WILL DROP

I MUST HAVE THE OCEAN IN MY HEAD

& IS A WHOLE
OF SHARPENED POINTED MOMENTS.

IF I AM CUT I PAUSE
BUT CANNOT WAIT.

OWL MEASURES IT: *LIE DOWN AGAIN*.

WINDOWS
HAVE ABSORBED DEATHSKIN

INFORMATION SWIMS THROUGH
AND MUST BE MARKED BY THIS FILTER

LIGHTFLOW / GASBREATH
LENS COATED BOTH WAYS

A NEW JOB ON THE MARSHLINE
OLD BOUNDARY

THE RING ABOUT THE FINGER OF HER WAIST
SQUEEZES PAINT FAT DELICATELY
RIPPLES RIPPLES, RIPPLES
TO A SMILE THAT DOESN'T SHOW

ANKLEBONE LOOPS INKY
OVER RIDGE OF HER BOOT

IMBALANCE TILTS WORLD PICTURE
PARTICULARLY CLOSING ON TV SOAP
OPERAS WHERE ATTENTION IS A FLICKER
NO HIGHER THAN GAS FLAME IN PAGODA

WE WERE DEAD AND WERE ABLE TO BREATHE

AND IN THE FORM OF BEARD
CLAY DOES HANG FROM HIS FACE

EYECRACK EXTENDING
TO THE VERY PLANT OF EAR

TWITCHES A FISH TO THE LIGHT
CHLOROPHYLL GREENGROW

MANDALA SPIDERWEB DIAGRAMS
MASK THE BLACK HOLE
FROM WHICH HIS HEART HAS WALKED

THE NAPHTHALENE DREAM

MARCH 16

A family drama enacted within the murk emulsion of some British Lion rationing comedy. This is a wax parquet come-dancing environment with foam mountains, where fever-blood pumps a steep graph of genetic theatre.

We scream to the root. And endure equally violent silences. It is all nightstuff and horsehair.

Sit facing west, the brass horizon, in a back-projection chariot rocked by a giant mechanical hand. Pale grandparents rise in fright. The old man shouting for the engine to be killed, pissing wild, gold stream blown back into our faces by the wind-machine. Hysterical goat-island laughter of other family members.

And then we are climbing out of the earth-bowl of a football stadium. Barefoot on stone steps. Swinging down a trellis of wires and girders, rusty vine shoots. Dropping softly to the ground. On monkey carpets.

The head of the valley. It is the mountain dream again. An outsize homage to John Ford, his blindness. Mythic cloud tiers of snow plaster, cut-outs of frontier cabins, takeaway Chinese décor in scarlet and gold. And two live albino bison: tethered, grazing.

Turn from this to the valley's heart. Prepare to descend.

One of my companions dives into a pool. I follow, my shoulder towards home, memory. A chain of ponds, connected. Follow him, clothed, swim across. The water is dark and thick with plant tangle. I cannot climb out so easily. The plants are lizards and snakes. Green and grey deaths swarming towards me. The rock that surrounds the pond is made from snakes, their bodies slide into cracks and fissures. They move their heads. Acid menace, time streaks.

Beneath, and to my left, is another, larger pond. Under the surface is a wheel or cog or mandala. Which is perhaps associated with our Hackney bathplug stopper. Or with the 8-spoked sun of the ogham stones. There are many more snakes. It is easy to sink, to descend into this second cooling-furnace pond. Other ponds are visible beyond that. The horror of the situation must increase. Snakes close about him. The problem is shelved in waking.

He remembers that the old man is Einstein.

COUNTING THE STEPS TOWARDS POLLEN

I dug
(& planted)
the sun

steam of kettle
half the garden / in shadow

lines of notebook words
cropt

dandelion heads break through this carpet
with rumours of sick coffee, bitter salads

when you aren't here, the kitchen blind

stays up

peeling black olives for a cat
slow & pretentious work

pain

jams a serrated blade
against the ball of my thumb

mind blocks this track

rainwater on biro tip

not a good run. to start

∎

solar mortar / sticker
is disc that draws the hand
and casts the shadow

in Cambridge, let's split
his profile sucked from a coin

sun sun / the sheer
                            leap

∎

plant, planet: semantic kinship

green codex

the information animals hold
& do not choose to transmit
in any other form
essential bodily actions

(here) fire trails calcify

■

sunflowers
this cap of bees
honey coats the explosion

seeds & pollen
the burst-potential
in the first grain

storage
in black earth
pods

■

weather's dog
shakes thunders

fleas from

the baby's
red-gash mouth

■

this garden corridor
atavistic impulses

dig with its head
Wolf Drill
spiralled for effective bite

chews out soil
shave worm & stone
dead bean shoots

in the tree's face
are motions of refusal

nobody owns green

■

his pearly / slime
mashed bloodroot

violation

raining
black pitch
of crushed insects,
metal glue & turpentine

no tent, the most obscure
field corner

where forced congress
can have no outcome

pieces (the boat painting)

∎

tree saliva
pollutes sight

ecstasy / unrepressed

yellow door
nailed across window hole

blank afternoon

        no.
I want to see it

■

water rupture
stains the polythene
morning sac

bodylice roll back skinstone

black rats, heated

sky has a clue not to be read

woken. the river tap

■

'grey, perishing light'

then rain, unintense

coughing the death of his chest
murdering his mornings

the printer is sick
words are still written

■

comatose tomato

words with clocks
wait in earth stations

nothing dramatic
lifts them into air

(kicking)

▪

swamped in wood saloon
        or public-
                taproom
Potman Wanted
      the official stance requires wine
         cough syrup
& flat beer
              (Wm Austin Balls of Bethnal Green Road)

mug faces
spray over the edge
of red tables
        dirty glasses

    his remarkable
           blue chip
        eyes

underdogs to the last man

the evening
papers the corridor

insects sound an empty house

▪

'he was no savage; a solitary'

meandering, urban
              and not in spectral
meditations

              carriage of base instincts
              through unpublic streets

and buying this loneliness
a hoard gently hoarded

      sound-mix

thought of others, in this

          celebrated

'poets as such, that is disciplined lives'

      eye on a leash:

          TARZAN DIES

■

walking into the kindly
whips of the wind

eyes cut by grit
imported on this storm

cedes blood / sneezes

skincarried micro-organism
lodging in his crack

aerial perspective
twists vortex through the noses
of dieting shopboys

the first gay athlete star

impressive themes are sprung
to sell newspapers

he, on the other hand, does not
'believe' in advertising

'it's funnier to bend things than to break them'

MAY 16

At St Pancras Old Church. Drawn against the
repetitive boredom of the pavements to investigate
the building, its slight eminence. And it is
unlocked, briefly, at this hour: 10.30 am.

    I encounter
               the vicar
hobbling on a stick, a Powys ghost.

    Empty church.
             Study some of the relics.

A woman emerges, shows St Augustine's stone
under the altar drapes: Kentish Rag. She talks.
    The curate
             left the church to work
at the hospital for nervous diseases. Had a brain
haemorrhage. Now paralysed down the left side. Has
faith in a cure. Gower Street say that they have
done all they can.

There is a subdued disapproval of the momentum
implied by his actions, as the woman narrates them.
    Today he is departing early, leaving her to
secure the building. He is to visit the Bishop of Durham
on a mission that has not been disclosed.
    This church is part of that northern rail, it drinks
from ancient Christian sources.

    The helper
                worries about vandalism. Children
give her 'a mouthful of language'. Lack of god
is her spider.

The place is cold and moulting. I purchase
a leaflet. Note several items.

> *About six feet down in the foundations of the old tower an altar stone was discovered minus its relics but clearly marked with five consecration crosses of curious shape. The form of the crosses is said to be unlike any other but that on the tomb of Ethne, the mother of St Columba, who died in 597. If this is so, it would seem to date the stone as late sixth or early seventh century, and point to a connection with Celtic Christianity via the kingdom of Northumbria which extended much further south than is usually realised.*

> (&)

> *The young Thomas Hardy, then an architect's apprentice, supervised the seemly carrying out of the last part of this work and perhaps gained there his ever-recurrent interest in churchyards.*

> (&)

> *Here P.B. Shelley, lodging at 5 Chapel Terrace (now blotted out by the railway arches), first saw and fell in love with Mary Godwin who was visiting her mother's grave.*

▪

In the evening we take a punt on Truffaut: *Anne & Muriel* or, *Les Deux Anglaises et le Continent*, at the Screen on the Green, Islington.	Anna recalls her dream of the previous night, connected with this imagery, which she finds 'tawdry'.

The dream was unpleasant
specifically, that she was making love in a red room

blood on the rumpled sheets, full screen

mouth choked with shit & vomit

'my mouth is full of earth'

Anne's dying remark, quoted...

                                        Other things.

Muriel sicks mud at the news that Anne & Claude have once been lovers.	The Brontë references, relating to Anna's instinct for & recent research into the mad sisters, our renting a cottage in Howarth.

The botched elemental tone of the proceedings
amplifies Anna's dislike of the two girls.

She could not know then that Truffaut
wanted Marina Warner to audition.

Rail mud splashes the lens. And remains.	Wales in Brittany. Her childhood holidays shot upon the supposed ground of my maternal ancestors.

... star prison, corona borealis

shame inks the evening window
as grape-coloured frames
dazzle in tungsten

television floats & flows
flickers, & also burns
revealing black holes
when significant matches
are struck

the brittle fragmentation is
anti-cubist, not at all
that kind of serial energy

no names, no dates
a pool of water under the set

RELATIONS IN THE MALE HOUSE

THE HILLS ARE CROWNING
RABBIT HEADS BREAK THROUGH WET GRASS

ILLICIT LOVERS
LICK & BITE

AWAY FROM HOME WE
CANNOT FUCK

TENDERNESS ALONG SPINE'S RIDGE
SUFFERS CHILD'S ICE FINGER

& HIS NIB WAS HARD
A FORM OF GRAPHITE

STRAINED TO MAMMAL SKY
30 DAYS OF HEAT
BONE POLLEN DUSTING ENGLISH LAWNS

BOOKS BURNT ON WIRE
THUNDER SHIELD / STRUCK

JUNE 14

FAMILY CLIMBS THE VALLEY OF DESOLATION.
PINE SHADOWS.
TRAIL MARKED WITH WHITE STONES.

IT BREAKS ONTO OPEN HILLSIDE, SPLITS.
A SMALL CAIRN DRAWS US TO THE LEFTHAND PATH.
THIS WAY WE STRIKE AT COW & CALF ROCKS.

OVER A CLEAR STREAM, THE BRACKEN.
FERN FRONDS TALL ABOVE BABY. HER GREEN FACE.
IT IS MY WHIM TO PLACE HER WITHIN A DUST CIRCLE.
TO CLOSE THIS TRAP WITH ANOTHER.
TO ADD SOME LOOSE STONES.

SUN SINKING.

AT THE FORK, A DEAD RABBIT STRETCHED
BEHIND THE CAIRN. ALREADY INVADED.
FLIES ARE PART OF THE RABBIT BODY.

ON RETURNING, TAPS OPEN. GUSHING BROWN.

BLISS OF NIGHT DEW
DAMPING NOSE BULB

TV LIGHTS
COBRAMILK MANTRAS

EXPERIMENTAL FILMMAKERS
BOIL THE EMULSION STAMPS

BY CAFFEINE DRINK
INTO BLACK CABBAGE

AT THE HEIGHT OF IT
A SALT TASTE

SCALPING TAKES THE LID OFF
PAIN-NERVE

SIMPLY, THE ACT OF
& JUST IN CASE

SUBTLE POLLEN PERSECUTIONS
RUST ON GRASS STALKS

SCYTHES & HOOKS SHARPENED
LIKE QUILLS
TO FLESH IN GREEDY NOSES

AND CAROL SAYS: EAT IT

'THEY DETERMINED TO CUT OUT THE TONGUES OF THE WOMEN, LEST THEIR LANGUAGE BE CORRUPTED'

USED CLOTHES
INSIST ON THE SEX ACT

TAUGHTNESS STRINGS HIM
HUNG FLESH IN NETS

THIS INJECTION
ON COUCH OR BED

DIPS HAND INTO GREASE POT
SMEARS HIS READINESS

DRESSED AGAIN
AND THE SUITCASE IS LOST

NAKED FIGURES WRESTLE THE TWILIGHT

HOT FACE A GATE OF BLOOD
(A STILE)
WITH ROCKS TO CARRY

THE PROMISE OF A STREAM
UNFULFILLED
IN MUD THAT'S HARD BAKED

'IF HE BUILDS A CORRUGATED
IRON SHACK, I'LL TEAR IT DOWN.
AND THAT'S TRIBALISM'

SO THEY FADE ACROSS REFECTORY TABLES
(THE DRUGGED AFTERNOON MOOD)

OUTSIDE A WINDOW GRILLE
BROWN FIELDS STRUGGLE

(STINKING ROOT CROPS)
BABY'S RUG COVERS SHARP STONES

THE MOON OF MAKING FAT

JULY 14

for Chris Torrance

       morning feet in mist

midge filters

dull thatch of conifer
overcommissioned land

           climbing into sleep

it is my dream & soaks my shoes
it is a turn to the right

soft magnet of ice
unearthing homeopathic roots

    toadstool (*panaeolus campanulatus*)
    pushes its conical helmet
    through crust of cowshit

    on the low Cymmer wall:
    FRANK ZAPPA CAPTAIN BEEFHEART

the railway station from which Robert Frank departed
now a pub (Welsh Brewers)
then going over the map's edge
to swoop on stick of sheep spine

something local to carry as totem

    ▪

Rhys, the neighbour farmer, generous, turn-eye:
'I know them to see, see, but I'm not acquainted'

leads me down through a damp woodclump

    springwaters
    gathered in a coke can & drunk

the bearded man rises from his circle

    dark, home-brewed beer
    mint-tasting silences

    his long-range weather
    perfectly accurate

night rain feeds the garden herbs

by starlight, 'together on speed', boils tea

    considered
    incidents of movement

an ancient Welsh profile breaks the door
'by the sweat of our brows shall we earn our bread'
dud left thumb clamps beer glass
slow drinker waiting on the 10pm murder news

TAXI GIRL FOUND IN MINESHAFT

& though his visit is 'disapproved of'
the farmer leaves the solid words

    ■

along the roadside
gravel shimmer, white stone margin

    dry rattle by water tank
        drill of sun
                  at zenith

bites into collar bone

sticks neck hair
dries skin into raw creases

steps upon the mountain dream
are treacherous, sucking boots down

    reverie,
       unsecured paths

Craig-y-Llyn, mother of glaciers

  ■

spreads vinegar, cold tea & mint
across burnt shoulders

'I knew the real was yonder
& the darkened dream of it was here'

pot of smoked salmon paste
buttery taste to grease disillusionment
nothing turned out as it was planned
the cupboard trophies hoarded
against future, silence

loses breath in cloud scarf
'the earliest example of freewill'

HYMNS TO NERGAL

WAITING FOR THE BONE LUNCH TO WORK
AND IT'S ALL A (VEGAS TYPE) GAMBLE

... COULD BLOW YOUR HEAD OFF
 BUT NOT HURT

LOOKING, VAINLY, FOR HIS PLACE
IN THE FAUNAL LIST

    ICE DIET BREEDS NEW EXCITEMENT
        THE AMINO CLUE
FURNISHED AN OPENING
    SO THAT A SOLO JOURNEY
        (TO THE SOUTH AGAIN)
BECAME A MYSTIC AMBITION

LET THEM ASSUME MOUNTAINS
AND I DO WALK
    IN RECOGNITION
    & TREAD OF TREMBLING DARKNESS

THAT YOUR BIRTH IS A FUSE
BURNING TO MY EXTINCTION

    YOU ARE
    WHAT IS NOT EATEN

& MAKE OF THIS CURVE OF LOVING

    NEW LIGHT

THE ENAMEL COOKER DOOR
A MAP OF THE CAT'S BLOOD

PLOTTING OBSCURE PLANETARY CONJUNCTIONS
THAT ARE OF HIS OWN MAKING

SOMEWHERE A SPACEFIELD
NOW EXISTS IN HIS NAME

FETID MINERALS OF FLIGHT
SNARLING PUNCTURED EAR FLAP

CAME INTO BEING TO CALIBRATE
ONE CELESTIAL SPLASH
& SO WITH OTHER LESSER ACTIONS
(UNMOTIVATED) BLOOD LETTINGS

FLAUNTED AS THREADS OF EYE
DANGLING DOWN A RIBBON OF CHEEK

A NEW THEORY FOR SERVETUS?

'LIKE A WIND THAT CHANGES ITS DIRECTION
AND THEREFORE ITS NAME'

STANDING ON THE THIN
                    SURFACE
                            FUSILLAGE
            OF TAPLOW GRAVEL

            MISSING THE ANKLEHIGH
            FLIGHTPATH OF INSECTRY

                    THE ZIZZZZZZZ

INDICATING DYNAMO CIRCUITS
ELLIPTICAL ORBITS
MADCAP BIKER ORGANIZATIONS

            THAT IT GOES ON

            THE LIFE OF

'THE DAY ENDED WHEN THE LIGHT BECAME YELLOW'

HAWKSTONE

RAIN ILLUSION THICKENS
ADDER'S-TONGUE FERNS HANG FROM MASONRY

A FINGER DRUMMING ON BEER CANS

HOW FAR DOES THIS GROW
FROM THE IMPOSSIBILITY OF USING A CAMERA

I MENTIONED THE STARS CREATED BY EGO
NOW I CAN ACTUALLY WATCH THEM MELT

PLANT TYPEWRITER TAPS OUT GARDEN EARTH
ROOT FINGERS RECORD ASTRAL INPUT

ANIMAL STEPS THROUGH QUIESCENT POLLEN
COUNTING YEARS BY PLANET BREATH

... HALF DEAD GALACTIC TRAILS...
CELL CODES COLOURING MANDEATH

ONLY THE ATOM REMEMBERS
THOSE LONDON CANNIBALS

GRASP A ROSE OF PALE FIRE
NETTLE TONGUES STING
THE ROOF OF HIS MOUTH

FORCE OPEN THE STAR LATTICE
SO THAT LIGHT CAN BEND
OUR STEPPED VERTEBRAL TOWER

PLUNGE THISTLE IN HOT OIL
A FRAMED EXHIBIT
TO CONJUGATE OR COOK

CIGARILLO SINGES MANBEARD

CRACKLE LIKE STATIC
A WELDING MYSTERY VIEWED
WITHOUT PROTECTIVE GOGGLES

(THEN THE ALBUMIN COUNT)

CLOTTING THE PASSAGES, SUN SPOTS
STENT FATTY TUNNELS

BECAUSE THE EQUATION COMES OUT
GALAXY EXTENDS HER FOOTAGE

JUNK METAPHORS TEST
BLACK ROOTS OF MOONLIGHT
BITTER CHALK ON CAPILLIARIES

RIBCAGE SKY PINKING
AS SOFT BONES PLUNDER

SHOOT TIME-DISSOLVING CHEMICALS
INTO HARD GAY BRUISES

ICEMAN COMETH

THAT WE ARE
PIECES OF GLACIER
STILL WALKING

TUBES OF CLEAR WATER
RETAINING CRYSTALLINE PIGMENTATION
OF ICE-MOTHER TONGUE

SHARP SPLINTERS OF ORIGIN
BROKEN OFF
SCRATCH THEIR STORIES

HOW SLAVE TO
SEASON'S IRRATIONAL JOLT

MURDER COLOURS SPLASH BIG SCREENS
UNAESTHETIC TO A FAULT

MANIA IS BLACK AND BUILDS
TISSUE FOR FRESH SCARS

A HOOF OF STARS HAMMERS AGAINST
THE LEASH OF BONDAGE COLLARS

PUNCH OF BONE TAKES OUT THROAT
SPEECH CENTRES TERMINALLY INHIBITED

WE'D EAT EARTH PUTTING SEA MILES
BETWEEN WHAT IS & WHAT MIGHT HAVE BEEN

SCREAMS KNIFE ZONES IN BRAINTREE
TOO SLIPPERY TO HOLD

REIN IT IN OR STAGE A YARD
OF JOHN GEORGE HAIGH (GRADE) SLUDGE

KEEP AWAY FROM MOORS & HEATHS
CAN'T ASPIRE TO THE 'COOL' OF EARTHWORMS

FROG KILLER MEMORIAL

The strange ever-changing light, the endless streets and the shuddering feel of the sprawling city lingers in my mind like a faintly glimmering memory of a long forgotten, perhaps never experienced childhood, which, if rediscovered and illuminated, would ameliorate the pain of the present.
    Leon Kossoff, 1973

AUGUST 10

here even the chickens in their cages
crowned red judicial
let out pieces of the sun

        morning cries, part of the setting
        the royal arch of myth

a shocking feathered whiteness

children of the ghetto drained of their oils
move about (exiled)
capped against corneal intrusions

        & the arcs of violence occur
        like sudden summer storms

an ox, out of himself, in stormy terror
stamps a density
between church pinnacles

        some temple algebra sealed off

they tear down the stone with pendulum
pins sucked from the masonry

        to recover the dream
        of an aboriginal dynamism

        re-enactment of emotions, ineradicable
        strong silent heat of august

twenty minutes from Thames-side
pouring ullage into a drain

11

the same photograph on different occasions

it was true all along
& is now seen to be
& fades back
an overexposed area

shooting from the shadows out
into an illuminated field

yellow: plant failing for iron

sun, thin & bloodless as moonshine

cat flattens to incubate carrot flowers

small small, the cheque
drawn against desire

the statement of the grass is sticky
& anyway not permitted

light (what happens) is fobbing

no occult protection

I resent the arrest that is still to come

III

it is not a stable universe
& we are not stable elements in it

moon floats dangerously
old forests sway & reach

even my knuckle bone, out of joint
tips the balance
& ruins the chemical description

we stumble, trip, damage ourselves
just this side of extinction

epidermic insect batteries
tick off their retail choices
on a list of chemical elements
looking for missing metals

arrow points out the direction
for the wind to travel (west always)

put enough accidents together
& someone has a new godhead

IV

    early light, cooling
visible through the vegetable city

        Spitalfields

          off-shoot colouring, straw
gathered around the hermetic needle
                  of Christ Church

    a working geometry!

THE ACT OF SEEING WITH ONE'S OWN EYES

to confront our raw meat identity
      greedy for image magic
that we are sinew & blood, cartilage
bone heraldry revealed
foul body cage cut open
      screams out its beauty

    to recognise the dead flesh

the last filaments of soul
are stretching blue
giving up their ghosts

    rain spores between paving cracks
    humanoid relics gather cardboard
    & rags, three-day beards
    clothe them

    & their skins are wood
    their feet nailed

'give him credit, boy, & you're dead'

HEART'S EYE: A TABLE TOP MANIFESTO

This is a declaration nailed to the desk of a rag trade millionaire. Locked in an office, somewhere above the already doomed parade of King's Road, dosed with champagne, and set before a large typewriter, the hireling poet is required to produce, within the hour, biker waiting to depart for the airport, a map of the culture. The bespectacled sculptor, chewing his fingernails, sits in the corner, hard against the wall, spitting out broken aphorisms.

From within the dull clay of an imagined centre, there must come the force of the new. We are no longer waiting on the edict of the pyramid: Arts Council, *Time Out*, BBC. Some snake-mouth, print-excreting giant sloth. Trust the reach of instinct's non-judgemental judgements: the nerves and cortex-bruising flashes.

What this means in practical (and workable) terms is an abandonment of lazy supplement-swallowing habit patterns, conditioned reflexes, media lists of worst and best; that ugly notion that art is a matter of statistics and bullet points, not a dithyrambic wail of celebratory rage. We do not want, or desire, new gods. We do not require the mystifications of a high cathedral culture, that kaleidoscope of paste-and-plastic superstars with more teeth and less bite. We must bring narrative back to the oldest forms, tribal earth-feasts still lodged inside our lizardly consciousness. We must notice, with birth-fresh eyes, the slow abrasion of dust on pupil: the cloud-wheel, the planting of crops, the reaping of harvests, the burning car on the motorway sliproad. We are all participants in the theatre of the street. Watch the watchers watching as they wait.

The inner eye of necessity swivels towards those who have already grasped the secret locked in every cell of our genetic coding. Cliché is sanctified by repetition. Throw whiskey once in the offender's face and you offend. Do it three times and you have drama. The low-energy manifestations of recent years are put aside as redundant. The force has been bled from such once buoyant ephemerals as *The International Times* and its cannier, mirror-licking succubus, *Oz*. No more obscenity trials, no more lawyers. They have broken the treaty of limitations with the period in which they operate. They have become, already, historical ghosts targeting curators and collectors.

We must look instead to such as Stan Brakhage, a film artist who has thrived on the eclipse of neglect. Rilke is wise when he advises poets to remain unknown: fame will destroy their sense of privacy, the source of their power. We should be content to work with the privilege of rejection. To ignore the calculations, histrionics, hesitations, and do-I-dares of the reality principle, the materialist safety anchor. As Brakhage, so abundantly, demonstrates: his *Songs* elevating the human and the domestic, shared warmth within the tribe, the circle of fire. The oldest movements, light to dark.

8mm celluloid visions of childbirth, animal death, lovemaking, are valid extensions of the home movie. LIGHT! A prismatic shimmer encourages the emulsion to burn and bleach. Image is layered over image to finesse glittering horizons, interior oceans, and star fields within a bead of sweat on the loved one's back. This is a true beginning and sets us off down the root and tube of Brakhage's ancestor-fears into the curled slumber of the cosmos. Not childbirth but starbirth, planetary parasites floating like pollen on the slow breath of wood-stained memory: *Dog Star Man*. The most basic mammal enterprise. A man climbs a hill to cut down a tree – and, in so doing, enters the corridor of archetypes, the maze of memory spectres. Beyond the chimera of cinema is a journey of risk to the edge of the corrupted city: heart surgery, quivering flesh, metal wombs, mortuary marble. The black script in which we are all implicated. The camera is made sacred and demystified. It is an instrument and an extension of eye and wrist. Anyone can use it. Do not rely on the authority of print. Your own partner, your ground: they will repay the rawness of attention. No more big-screen politics, no more serpent finance. DO IT, WITHOUT CALCULATION: TO DISCOVER FOR YOURSELF JUST WHAT IT IS.

The scanner sweeps the screen, revealing new columns of words; language stripped back, traced to source, dazzling etymologies. Those who listen are those who will be listened to: Charles Olson – whose awkward and terrible seizure of the roots of history and legend, the power summoned to carry out this task, made unsustainable demands on his body and being. His life / his work. Others follow the trails he has broken. Edward Dorn astride his *North Atlantic Turbine*. J. H. Prynne whose still underappreciated texts are scrolls of witness for our times: *The White Stones, Brass, Into the Day*. And back, though he has never gone away, to the chartered streets, to the hot metals and mineral prophesies of Blake. Place as an adjunct of vision. Walks undertaken. Arrangements of old stones as broken metaphors.

Test your own responses to what you find, what they want you to see and appreciate. Interrogate the curation of Richard Long's retrievals, his tactful records of epic hikes, because the essence of the journey is not to be found in a photograph or the spiral on a gallery floor. Some measure of sympathy is discovered, among the fashionistas and uneasy weekend celebrities, for the dream umbrella of Carl Gustav Jung: 67,000 lakeside visions. Academics retrace Black Mountain College experiments in living-as-education. History factored through geography, not textual propaganda or arbitrary sponsorship. Old magicks are dusted down to receive new credit from rock stars and junk-pit scavengers: alchemy, astrology, prophecy. The sacred burn of vision is found within the bread-and-water rituals of everyday life. Symmetries of bud and shell. We can interbreed with intelligent machines. It need not be rape. Technologies do not have to be disposable and we are not compelled to elevate them into a new priesthood. A religion without priests and prophets. A commonwealth without parliaments. A realm without kings and courtiers. Where the idiot shaman leads the dance.

What does the sculptor, unpicking his V-necked Fair Isle sweater, say, as he squats in his corner? The biker is already rapping at the door. I tap out the last words from his urgent stutter.

The membrane begins to rend with fatigue. Volcanic energies underneath filter up. The city is still alive. The obscure and the deserted are safely encapsulated in disinterest. The random ektachrome eye cannot digest the intense value of these psychic histories. Amid grey motives and stained processes, the thinking mind, in its power, cuts through dilettante tendrils and refocuses our blank somnambulist into the beam of total consciousness.

SATURNINE GRAVEYARD KARMA

NOVEMBER 18

on such a day the trees are seen
as sealed umbrellas and we do not
smell the rain of sky vapours cirric
whispering overhead

growth here is fast we are
comfortable our dim thoughts cherish
their own exhaustion in trees & roots
the grids are set against an
invalid's flushed sunset

gas is tired our coats
are black only the child is
unaffected her red boots stamp
chaotically the clinging leaf mould

much local stone is gone under
the central mass the church
is finished such flowers
as there are fall in with
the whole In Memoriam (A.H.H) mood

this woman walks through in a grey
length holds fire to her breast
protection the candlepower is weak
& frost closes immediately outside
the gate its marks are cut into
the grass verge a hansom waits at
the curbside but do not think
we can enter this willing suffocation

rhizomorphic fibres cancel the nightmare

NOVEMBER 19

sick flesh no trace of pigment infolds
the plaster frog is cracked he
lifts his winter gun welsh air
compressed & oily stabs through
the green waterproof of their skins
'subtle patterning' dredges
corpses by the bucketful

no light around this tank
grey inhalations
appletree tangle overspreads lush grass
king's oak is a dud candle
acorn mulch layers the pond

conditions breed up nothing new
the gunman is incredulous a child

in the next valley they debate granite
for an uncut memorial stone

the text will be simple
name date & next of kin

DECEMBER 8

full moon; THE EYE
                OF THE BODY
     CANNOT BEAR

     ... stuck in the craw
     colourless & sore, both

battered submission
as it runs
congealed thing
lodged in his throat

THE KIND OF TIME NOT TO AVOID

     in his throat
     like a bird's wing

     sepulchral winter season
     drew metaphors out

     not blood, but the soft thick
     dealing of lungs
     haunted his confessional

inert powder on cheek ink
pulling his eye from its socket

face made up
a Bowie menstrual mask

moon now fills like an hourglass
with density of feather chalk

YOU ARE PREPARED

FOR THE SHOWDOWN OF THE YEAR

says *Astra Nova*

THE MARS / URANUS OPPOSITION IS A MONSTER
& IT CUTS ACROSS TWO HIGHLY SENSITIVE
AREAS OF YOUR SOLAR HOROSCOPE

       Carol quotes fragments
       from a postscript
       which is itself fragmentary,
       New York Times

IN SPITE OF ALL THIS APPARENTLY
DEPRESSING INFORMATION JUPITER IN
AQUARIUS SHOULD SUSTAIN & COMFORT

       don't run into
       any more concrete
       pillars, keep
       those mailbags coming

still willing to play it, sam

strangle the railway
bury the proleptic pulse

as the whole child witnesses

A NOTE ON THE WHY
& WHEN OF IT

RED EYE is accidental archaeology (it shouldn't be here in this form, a perky ghost sleepwalking through streets first witnessed many years ago, tired veins shot with yellow and red inks). Sequences, now dusted down and assembled, were written in 1973 and prepared for publication by Albion Village Press in 1974. The typescript, on examination, proves to be an extension of the compulsive 8mm diary-filming that informed communal life in Hackney after 1969. Cameras were clapped out with overuse and rough handling and would be gone within a year or so. Set aside, so that Albion Village Press could run with *Acrospirical Meanderings in a Tongue of the Time* by Chris Torrance and *Vorticegarden* by B. Catling, this long thin typescript, comfortably lost among the detritus of the period, now stands revealed as an attempt to record the particulars of domestic life (house, garden, new child), by testing the limits of the tight circle of locality. Here is casual evidence of the beginnings of the wilder topographic speculations of *Lud Heat*, the skulking in churchyards, the tramps towards stone circles. Darker imperatives, the gothic nudge of developers and celebrity villains of every stamp, set *RED EYE* aside.

I wonder about this thing. Is it merely bloodshot after too many sleepless nights? Or flashed so harshly in brute exposure that performers look like vampires? A cheap whiskey to wash out contact lenses? A shoulder-launched missile? I think of something Jeremy Prynne wrote, after witnessing one of those strange 8mm films. He speaks of being looked at by the image on the screen, 'a history prophesied in its own making'. He quotes Hawking on the de Sitter system: 'in this space there are closed curves, non-homotopic to zero, on going round which the orientation of time is reversed'. 'The resulting possibilities for causal imprisonment are the familiar star trap we have already witnessed,' he concludes. And that says it, everything the lost book, coming awkwardly into the light, might try to fix.

Some of the poems were originally published, in earlier versions, in *Grosseteste Review* and *Turpin*. Publication in book form is entirely due to the energies of Test Centre who have returned Hackney to a state of readiness and experimental action, both ways in time.

RED EYE by Iain Sinclair

Published by Test Centre in 2013 in an edition of 500 copies. Of these, 50 copies are numbered and signed, and 26 hardbound copies are lettered, signed, and contain additional holograph material and a DVD. There are also 7 copies *hors commerce*.

Text & images copyright © Iain Sinclair

Designed by Traven T. Croves

Printed by Lecturis, Holland

Fiction + poetry submissions encouraged for reproduction in indeterminate form and circulation. Everything still permitted. Auto / collage / cut / mail / repairs / writ / transcript

Send SSAEs for information to Test Centre, 77a Greenwood Rd, London E8 1NT

www.testcentre.org.uk

ISBN
978-0-9926858-0-5 (paperback)
978-0-9926858-1-2 (hardback)